inspire a dream • inspire a dream • inspire a dream •
inspire a dream • inspire a dream • inspire
inspire a dream • inspire a dream • inspire a dream •
inspire a dream • inspire a dream • inspire a
inspire a dream • inspire a dream • inspire a dream •
inspire a dream • inspire a dream • inspire a
inspire a dream • inspire a dream • inspire a
inspire a dream • inspire a dream • inspire a dream •

dedicated to

all the people who

INSPIRE A DREAM

HONOR
BOOKS

Inspire a Dream

ISBN 1-56292-849-X
Copyright © 2000 VisionQuest Communications Group, Inc.
and Koechel Peterson & Associates

Published by Honor Books
P.O. Box 55388
Tulsa, Oklahoma 74155

Research, Information, and Transcriptions:
Mary Ann Van Meter, LeAnn Fisher, Annette Glavan, Lori Matheny,
Alyssa Garrett, Jennifer Lewellen, Ruth Menefee, and Diane Fisher

Text Editing: Lance Wubbels and John Humphrey

All quotes from current players are taken from interviews conducted
for various VisionQuest programs and projects.

This book in its entirety is the creation of Koechel Peterson & Associates
in partnership with VisionQuest Communications Group, Inc.

Photography by Tom Henry *(unless otherwise noted)*

Barry Sanders, Tom Landry: Jonathan Daniel /ALLSPORT
Junior Seau: Jed Jacobsohn /ALLSPORT
Youth, Cris Carter, Mark Brunell, Kyle Brady: Andy Lyons /ALLSPORT
Deion Sanders: Ezra O. Shaw /ALLSPORT

"Life is itself but a game of football."

SIR WALTER SCOTT

FOREWORD

Dreams. We all have them. Many of us are driven by them.

A mother dreams of a better life for her child. The child dreams of making his mother proud, her efforts successful.

Many people dream their lives will count for something more than punching a time clock and bringing home a paycheck.

Our dreams help define us and our futures. A wise king once said, "As a man thinks within himself, so is he." If we see our dreams as attainable, we push forward and become the very embodiment of the dream itself. And in so doing, we inspire others to dream as well.

The men on these pages have discovered that with God on their side, nothing is impossible. A dream germinated in them during their childhood while they played, as Darrell Green calls it, "a kid's game." And that seed became the impetus for their future, inspiring them to break the tackles of drugs, gangs, crime, poverty, broken homes, and self-doubt.

These men have risen above the pressures, demands, and challenges of the game—and life—to fulfill their destinies while serving as shining examples of virtue. Because of that, you and I have been blessed to witness these men perform to a high standard of excellence for sixteen or more Sundays each fall. They have thrilled us, amazed us, made us cheer, and inspired us to dream ourselves.

As a child a dream was planted in me; one that seemed a long way off. Yet I believed that by the grace of God I could get there. I've encountered hurdles and bumps in the road throughout my journey, but I've found that it really isn't the dream that brings fulfillment but rather the relationships developed en route that give meaning to life.

The men on these pages exemplify that. They show us that through faith, courage, and determination, our dreams are never too far away. And that as we nobly reach for them, we can inspire others to do the same.

JAMES BROWN
FOX NFL Sunday, Studio Cohost

"When you're a little kid, you dream about holding

the trophy up after throwing the winning touchdown

or scoring the winning touchdown. This is

what it's all about. It's what we've

played for all these years."

KURT WARNER

"Winning is why we do what we do.
We play the game to win. We play
the game to finish what we've started."

AENEAS WILLIAMS

PREGAME

PREGAME

"Everybody who is in the NFL was an all-American. Everybody was a superstar in high school. It's the guys who can prepare mentally who are the ones who have the edge."

IRVING FRYAR

The dream begins the first time a child smells a new leather football and is fueled by his first wobbly spiral, first diving catch, first shoestring tackle. It grows as countless eight-year-olds gallop across worn green fields or dusty vacant lots and leap into makeshift end zones, imagining themselves as Troy Aikman, Barry Sanders, or Jerry Rice making the big play in the big game and raising the victor's trophy.

All across America, from the inner cities to the heartland, on sun-drenched playgrounds and snow-covered yards alike, the dream lives on. Under Friday-night lights, high school stars picture themselves as soon-to-be pro football heroes. The Saturday afternoons of fall provide the landscape on which daydreams are painted for every would-be All-American who envisions a day when his name will be called in the NFL draft.

Football truly has become the American game. And with that, being a football star has become an American dream.

No sport has captured the imagination of the American people like football. And the dreams are not limited to youth. Even armchair quarterbacks dream of standing on the sidelines, creating new strategies, and calling plays. Fantasy team owners dream of overseeing franchise rosters, making trades, and building champions. Weekend warriors dream their waistlines svelte, their arms lively, and their legs swift as they propel their teams to victory.

From corporate "game plans" to classroom "teamwork" to giving a child a "time out," this sport has influenced us all. And in most cases, it has inspired a dream. Whether it's winning the biggest battles, overcoming the biggest challenges, outsmarting the biggest enemies, or making up the biggest deficits, football inspires us to dream big.

The dream is about a team in Tampa going 0-16 one year, and three years later playing for the NFC title.

The dream is about a brash young quarterback from Broadway guaranteeing a Super Bowl win, then backing up those words on the field, and, in doing so, delivering not only the win but the future of the league itself.

The dream is about a gray-haired 48-year-old trotting onto the field to boot yet another field goal for the Oakland Raiders.

"It's what gets you out there in the mornings to lift weights when you're in high school and keeps you after practice throwing the football when you're in high school. It's a dream, and I finally reached that dream. It's a great thrill."

TRENT DILFER

The dream is about a young gun from Denver directing his team 98 yards to glory in the last two minutes with no time outs.

The dream is about a San Francisco receiver corralling a pass with his fingernails to begin a 49er dynasty.

The dream is about a backup quarterback in Buffalo bringing his team back from 31 points down at halftime to a playoff win.

The dream is about a Pittsburgh rookie scooping up a deflected pass, millimeters from the turf, and churning 50 yards to pay dirt.

The dream is about a 28-year-old quarterback rising from football oblivion—and stocking shelves in a grocery store—to lead the St. Louis Rams to a Super Bowl championship, setting passing records and writing the most improbable story in NFL history along the way.

The dream is about what we are not yet, but can become.

Football gives a city and its people a team to hang a dream on. In football, more than any other sport, teams define the identity of their city. Pittsburgh's Steelers of the 1970s epitomized the blue-collar work ethic of the steel mill city and provided a rallying point in a depressed economy. The 49ers of the 1980s carried the flare and panache that makes the "city by the bay" a haven for visitors. For twenty-five years, the Cowboys held the swagger and pride that revealed the "biggest and best" attitude of Dallas and made the Cowboys "America's Team."

Only football brings fans out with barbecue grills and lawn chairs to fill parking lots in cities like New Jersey and Green Bay—four to five hours before kickoff. Only football ignites fans at the very back of the end zone in Washington to cheer as if they were front and center on the 50-yard line. Only football draws out shirtless, potbellied men in December . . . in Buffalo. Only football leads seemingly normal people to, for some undiscovered reason, paint themselves in the multicolored hues of their beloved teams.

All of this results from the pursuit of a dream.

"What's really great is just being out there with the teammates, the people you care about. If you take away all the press and glory, that's what's really fun."

ANTHONY JOHNSON

Football is built upon the dreams of those who heard over and over that they were merely dreamers with no real hope. It's about people like Mike Singletary who was told he was too small to ever make it big. It's about players such as Steve Largent who was told he was too slow to excel. It's about men like Kurt Warner who was told he didn't have what it takes to play at a professional level.

These are men who have been inspired by a dream and, in turn, inspired others to dream with them and follow. They prove that true champions are not swayed by circumstances, labels, or past experiences, but rather are driven by a force within that pushes them to become something greater than they could have become by themselves. They are men who inspire us to push beyond our own limitations to reach our destiny.

Buoyed by faith, courage, and determination, these men play the game for more than accolades or achievement. They play to give their all, to leave everything on the field, to stand as examples—men who are among the best at their chosen skill and who perpetuate the undying heart of a champion.

A dream is kindled in us as we watch, admire, and appreciate these true champions who have inspired a dream for this generation and beyond.

"It is an aggressive game. It's a game of collisions. But I see stories in the Bible of great warriors like David. It's something you can do with all your heart, and after the game is over, you can shake a man's hand and say that's a great job."
KYLE BRADY

"When I saw how much my own children idolized people across different segments of our society, I was struck by the kind of influence I can have over children's lives. All professional athletes are role models. The choice you have to make is whether you're going to be a good one or a bad one."
STEVE LARGENT

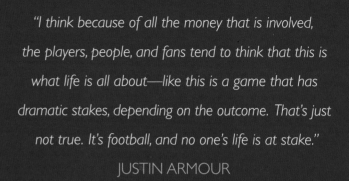

"I think because of all the money that is involved, the players, people, and fans tend to think that this is what life is all about—like this is a game that has dramatic stakes, depending on the outcome. That's just not true. It's football, and no one's life is at stake."
JUSTIN ARMOUR

"At times, it can be a very miserable profession. There's a lot of pressure and pain. But there are many times you look and think, Man, I have been so blessed. I get to play a game for a living."
MARK SCHLERETH

RUNNING BACKS

"Being physically smaller than everyone else,
or shorter, you have to have an edge. I think God's
given me the inner drive to want to work hard.
He's given me the ability to make people miss.
Because that's one thing I don't want to do is absorb
a lot of hits. If you've seen me run, I'd rather run
around a guy than run through him."

BARRY SANDERS

Is there anything so breathtaking in all of sports as watching the preeminent backs run to daylight?

Our minds drift to snapshots of Barry Sanders escaping a horde of Chicago Bears with one seemingly impossible move that leaves six grown men grasping at air and looking for a trace of the Houdini-like figure who was there one second, gone the next.

We see Emmitt Smith accelerating through the slightest hole and streaking down the sidelines to pay dirt.

. . . Gale Sayers, with two good knees, hurdling a 6'7" defensive lineman and then turning on the afterburners.

. . . Jim Brown brushing off tacklers like mosquitoes on his way to another first down.

. . . Walter Payton giving his all, and seemingly more, to turn a two-yard loss into a work of art.

. . . Earl Campbell, a runaway locomotive, leaving shoe prints on the jersey of a Rams' tackler.

. . . Curtis Martin, after his thirty-eighth carry of the game, picking his bruised and bloodied body up off the turf one more time to enter the huddle and ask for the ball again.

. . . Marshall Faulk, Terrell Davis, Robert Smith, Edgerrin James, and others still yet to make their marks.

"Run to daylight."

VINCE LOMBARDI

"Imagine if you had practiced playing, and God is standing

beside you. You know how hard you would try! That's the

way I feel. So, that's what really, really drives me."

CURTIS MARTIN

Running backs are supremely gifted athletes, who on one play assume the role of workhorse, and on the next that of game breaker.

These men are fearless. Tough. Quick. Graceful. Fast. Powerful. Elusive.

They run with the ball the way little boys do in their dreams—spinning, sidestepping, cutting, changing pace, pivoting, with sudden bursts and an uncanny knack for breaking tackles and making people miss. They fake and juke with such adeptness, even the best tacklers can be made to look foolish. Slipping and weaving through a broken field, dodging and ducking, they run around defenders as if they were orange street cones and over them like speed bumps. They refuse to be brought down, fighting for the extra yard as if their lives depended on it.

They possess vision beyond the norm and the ability to think two defenders ahead and react instantaneously. They change directions quicker than an SUV (and get better mileage). They can turn a simple plunge up the middle into a 60-yard touchdown. They sprint down the field and accelerate away from pursuit with the speed of a cheetah running away from its captor—even in the fourth quarter.

They make us shake our heads and ask, "How did he do that?"

Running to daylight is what it's all about for the best backs. The fewer the touches from defenders means the more real estate covered and the greater chance for longevity.

"I definitely thought I could score every time I touched the football. And oftentimes I did. So that gave you a kind of a premise that you were invincible."

MERCURY MORRIS

"Everyone wants to be recognized, but I'm very content to sit in the background and feel good that I played and blocked well in a game. I have enjoyment from the things I did on the field."

ANTHONY JOHNSON

FULL BACKS

"I used to score a lot of touchdowns, and now I'm begging to get one or two. But I'm happy with my role. I understand what my role is. Earlier in my career I had to understand that what was going to keep me in this game was to be a blocker."

HOWARD GRIFFITH

And what of this man, the fullback? This glorified battering ram. Is there anyone on the field with such a thankless job? He leads his running mate into the hole to clear out a path, thus constantly experiencing what it is like to dash into a wall from ten feet away. The fullback's job is to run full speed into either a 320-pound slab of defensive lineman who seems planted in the turf like a tree, or into an onrushing, hyperactive, salivating linebacker who is feeling rather aggressive and has been waiting for the last five plays for someone to body slam. Take your pick, thank you very much.

The fullback is all about sacrifice. He only dreams of being the featured ball carrier. If the offensive coordinator feels generous, the fullback might carry the ball once or twice. He will almost never see his name in the paper or show up on the highlight reel, but he is vital to the success of the team. If he misses an assignment, the result is lost yardage, a sack, or a stopped drive; or even worse, a fumble or injury.

He doesn't play for personal glory. He plays for victory. He is the ultimate team player.

"Whenever one person is down or someone is struggling,

everybody else kind of picks it up. That's what a team is.

A team is a whole group of guys who all work together

to accomplish something."

BOB CHRISTIAN

"I've got to go out and be motivated. I've got to work harder than ever. Because this is precious. What God has given me is precious."

IRVING FRYAR

RECEIVERS

RECEIVERS

He is like a gazelle, moving with unmatched grace and agility. He is pure speed, burning high-octane fuel—4.3 on the watch and rarely caught from behind.

He has a pair of venus flytraps extending from both arms, with the ability to latch on to balls like a passing meal.

He is Baryshnikov in pads, dancing around his stage with premium athleticism and unparalleled body control. No one athlete turns the game into pure poetry like the receiver. Often, he steals the show.

"Even at a very young age, I could play with the older guys. Even though I was the smallest guy, I could excel. But I'm still reaching. I'm still grabbing it. I'm still letting Him know I'm not satisfied. I know I can do better."

ISAAC BRUCE

"Not only did everybody else wonder if I could even play in the NFL, but so did I. When I came out of college, the prototyped wide receiver was about 6'3" or 6'4" and could run under 10 flat in the hundred, and I wasn't that. But there were a lot of things I could do well, and I was fortunate to end up with a team that was willing to take advantage of the things I did well."

STEVE LARGENT

Since I was a little kid, I always wanted to make the great catch.
Even when playing with my friends, if they threw the ball deep,
I would slow down so I could dive for it. I would always pretend
I was making a great catch. So, now that professionally
I'm able to do it, it's something I enjoy to do. But I
would much rather make an easy catch than
a spectacular catch. It just happens."

"Early in my career, I didn't put nearly as much
time and effort into my work as I do now.
Getting cut really made me work hard.
I expect a lot out of myself.
I know what I'm capable of doing.
That's the reason why I get up at six in the morning
and work out. Success is based upon getting
the most out of what God has given you."

CRIS CART

"I believe that almost every ball is catchable. A lot of the great catches I've made, I never thought I'd catch them. What I try to do is stop the ball—the point of it. Sometimes there's kind of a sweet spot. If I'm able to grab that spot on the football, I feel I can control it or bring it in."

The receiver's role is that of game breaker. No one can reach out and grab the momentum and turn it to his team's favor any quicker. If he can slip by his defender, he is, in a word, *gone*.

Stretching and leaping for balls that seem out of human reach, he is football's acrobat. He fearlessly goes across the middle of the field and sustains vicious hits, yet comes back to trespass that territory again.

He thrives on the big play. He gets up for the challenge of being double covered. He finds the open spot, ignores the two men hanging on his back, and lays out, giving up his body for the sake of a first down. He knows how to break tackles and become another running back after the catch.

He runs routes of precision. He zigs while defenders zag. He goes when defenders stop, and stops when they go. He scores while defenders watch.

In his dreams, he makes the winning catch in the Super Bowl, again and again.

He is the receiver, the most feared weapon in the game.

TIGHT ENDS

He is an enigma. Is he another lineman? Yes. Is he a receiver? Yes.

So which is it? What is he?

Well, both.

"To catch a winning touchdown pass, that would be great. But I want to affect this game wherever I am needed. When they have need of big plays, when they have need of a guy to come in and block a defensive end, I just want to be in a position to do what I can to help this team."

JACKIE HARRIS

He is a hybrid. A man who needs the temperament to block down on a 300-pound defensive end on one play and have the ability to catch the deep ball on the next. He needs hands tough enough to ward off a sack artist, yet soft enough to snag a pass at the sideline.

His assignments are multiple —blocking, running routes, decoying, going in motion, catching—and each has a significant purpose. Yet in the eyes of the public, he is typically the forgotten man.

The tight end is the combo guy in the warehouse. He works two full-time jobs, but gets paid for only one. He is football's version of the guy who grabs his lunch pail and hard hat, punches the time clock, and labors at his assigned tasks, day in and day out.

"I try to keep myself on an even keel, and I do a lot of praying. Just try to stay calm and relaxed. And then when Sunday gets here, it's time to let all the adrenaline out and the emotions run free. I go out and just be a crazy animal on the field, just let it all go."

ERNIE CONWELL

OFFENSIVE LINEMEN

They are bodyguards . . . there to "serve and protect" their more glamorous teammates—the quarterbacks and running backs. Theirs is a game of hand-to-hand combat, sacrificing their bodies—and recognition—for the success of the men behind them. They battle in the trenches through blood and sweat and tears, through pain and humiliation, until the job is finished.

Like sumo wrestlers with mammoth 300-plus-pound bodies, these warriors slam into their opponents play after play. Sixty or 70 plays of pounding the same man, trying to find some way—any way—to keep him out of the backfield. Grab, trip, push, tackle—but don't get caught. Under the pile, eyes are gouged, shins kicked, fingers bitten. Anything goes. By the time they walk off the field at game's end, linemen have been head slapped so many times, the migraines quickly escalate.

"It hurts a little more than it used to, but I probably take it a lot more seriously now, because I know that every time I go out there I'm that much closer to never playing again. And that's kind of an unnerving thought for me, because I've been playing this game since I was a kid."

BRUCE MATTHEWS

They are noticed only when they fail. False start, illegal formation, personal foul, holding—all bring bright yellow flags from referees and jeers from onlookers. Being beaten for a sack makes them bums. It is the only position that is best when not seen or heard about. Playing the offensive line can, at times, be truly offensive, and nearly always thankless.

Running backs will occasionally buy them a steak dinner. Quarterbacks will reward them with Rolex watches. But honor and glory are not what these men seek. For them, it's simply about keeping their teammates unscathed.

"You can go out and dominate the guy you're playing against. You can put him on his back 50 plays in a row ... then it can be third down and ten, and you need a completion to get into field goal range, and he beats you for a sack. He's the hero and you're the goat."

MARK SCHLERETH

"You can learn a lot from adversity. Adversity can make you stronger. It can bring a team together, or it can divide a team."
MARK BRUNELL

HALFTIME

HALFTIME

Football is a game of inches. An inch too much turns a long touchdown into just another incomplete pass. An inch too little and an interception is turned into a touchdown. Inches can mean the difference between victory and defeat.

At halftime, a team may find itself significantly behind. Perhaps the game plan hasn't been executed properly and every attempt at success has been countered. Failure hangs over the locker room as a menacing demoralizer.

So it is with life.

"You lose games and you're 0 and 5, and you start thinking you're the first guy to get fired and have never won a game! But the great thing about being a Christian and knowing that God is in charge is to know I was going through that for a purpose. Adversity can make you even better. I think 0 and 5 did that for our football team, and I think we won some Super Bowls because of it."
JOE GIBBS

"There was a point in my life when I tried to take my own life. At that point, I was involved with drugs, making wrong decisions, not being a good husband or father, winding up in the papers and in jail. As I sat in that jail cell, bleeding and cold, Jesus came to me and said, 'I don't care what it is you've done. I don't care how bad you feel about yourself. Here I am.' I looked up and Christ was there for me. No way in the world I could have brought myself out of the mess I was in."

IRVING FRYAR

But halftime provides a chance to reflect on what has taken place. It's an opportunity to assess the situation and gain perspective. One can make adjustments, develop new strategies, and regain composure.

We must strive to put aside the past and look ahead. The game is not over yet. There is still another half to be played. Setbacks can be turned into building blocks for a victory to come.

The dream can still be realized.

"I opened my eyes and saw my wife crying. She said, 'You just had a heart attack and died.' The doctors told me, 'Your football career is over. You had a massive heart attack, and you had some serious heart damage.' That changed my life. Before that, I thought nothing could hurt me, nothing could stop me; I could do what I want."

TONY JONES

"They went in and saw the blockage, and we went right into the open-heart surgery. Going through that made you aware of the things you take for granted. I never had any fear of dying. As a Christian, you understand that there is life after death. But I think also you have an attitude that when you go into something like surgery, it's almost like a football game. You go in expecting to win. I felt like God was with me."

DAN REEVES

"My mother wanted me to do something in a safe environment, so I ended up playing football. A lot of my friends were getting killed. My grandmother and my mother's sister were killed. My best friend got his chest blown out. I can go on forever about people who died— twenty friends or so. But that's what I believe turned me around and encouraged me to develop the relationship with God that I have. I always figured, why not me? As many times and as close as it's been, I know I escaped. I've grown a lot stronger because of that."

CURTIS MARTIN

DEFENSIVE LINEMEN

Across the line is the attacker, the pursuer, the hunter. He relentlessly beats on his opponent, doing anything to wear him down. He strong-arms, he darts, he clubs, using any means necessary to break free—like a man trying to avoid an ambush. The sack is his medicine. Making a quarterback hurt or a running back wish he had chosen a different path, his panacea. Being denied only heightens the fury with which he attacks. His motor never stops. When he succeeds, he lets everyone know— thrusting his arms skyward, sometimes adding a victory dance. Seeing that makes an offensive lineman sick.

"When I was younger, I was short and fat and got picked on. I was cut from the football team and instead played in the marching band. But I always had a dream to actually play. I grew from 5'8" to 6'3" in about six months. Once I got my height, I thinned out and started to play football. So, from there, it's almost as though it was God's will for me to be good in football."
KEVIN CARTER

"In combat, you're putting your life on the line. Looking back on some of the offensive linemen whom I go up against, it's like putting your life on the line at times."
CHAD HENNINGS

He has earned the right to become part of groups like
the "Fearsome Foursome," the "Purple People Eaters,"
the "Steel Curtain," or the "Sack Exchange," and to
receive a nickname like "Mean Joe" or "Big Daddy." He
is an offensive lineman's recurring nightmare.

He dreams of getting to the quarterback on every play,
yet doing so can be like navigating a living obstacle
course. He is frequently double-teamed and constantly
held, or so he says. Chuck the tackle, go around the
guard, hurdle the fullback, then chase the quarterback,
and he just might get there. Often it's only a tease,
arriving at the quarterback's face a split second after the
ball is released. Hit the quarterback then, and he'll surely
be flagged, maybe even fined. Frustration is the name
of his game.

Yet satisfaction comes with one play that can shift
momentum and change the outcome of the game—a
tackle for a loss, a fumble caused, a throw hurried, or a
key sack.

Then he can dance.

LINEBACKERS

LINEBACKERS

"Be consistent, play aggressive, play fast, and be disciplined."

CORNELIUS BENNETT

He is like a heat-seeking missile. Zero in on the target. Seek and destroy.

Linebackers are fearless explosions of controlled fury. They have a singleness of focus on their mission—to demolish the opposing ball carrier. They are determined nothing will stop them. Covered in mud and blood, knees aching, heads pounding, shoulders throbbing, they play on.

Linebackers are the people you don't want to meet at the end of a dark alley.

"We're the tempo-setters. No matter how big the game is, you can't go out there and wish for good things. You have to go out there and make it happen. I play all my games hard and physical. I just can't wait to make a big play and create some havoc."

JESSE TUGGLE

"When I first played middle linebacker in the seventh grade, my coach told me, 'You'll have to be the roughest guy on the field, but still be responsible for all the other guys on the field.' From then on, to me the role of middle linebacker was to assume leadership on the field. When I left the field, I wanted everything to be left on the field."

MIKE SINGLETARY

"I want to rock his world, but I never want him to get hurt. Coming from the blind side, you just de-cleat him, that's what you just always dream of. Hitting somebody so hard that you knock the wind out of them or their helmet flies off."

BRYCE PAUP

Butkus. Lambert. Nitschke. Singletary. Seau. The mere mention of the names brings a chill to the most veteran player. Head-on collisions with these men result in what looks like a rough night at the demolition derby.

The linebacker is the quarterback of the defense. He must study and know his opponents' tendencies. What formation gives away what play? What side will they go to? He must meet the center or fullback head on, shuck him like corn, then stop the oncoming freight train known as a ball carrier. As well, he must read the play fake and quickly drop back into pass coverage. Watch for the tight end or back over the middle. Read the screen and the draw, watch for the reverse—stay at home and don't be fooled.

"You have to pray. You have to be totally focused and determined to sacrifice whatever it takes to get there. When I am on the football field, I am at peace, and the peace comes from the Man upstairs. I have been given many individual accolades. I've been through a lot of hype. There is just so much involved before you get there, that when you get there you just better glorify God."
JUNIOR SEAU

"When I'm out there on the field, I'm out there to do my job. Just because you're a Christian, it doesn't mean you can't line up out there and try to knock somebody into next week."
GREG LLOYD

Not everybody is going to win. There's going to be a loser. The quest is how are you going to come back if you lose? Are you going to be negative and start complaining? Or are you going to take it to anoth level and anticipate the next game, turning it into a positive?"

JIM SCHWARTZ

Ten, fifteen, even twenty times a game, it is the linebacker who makes the tackle. He is like a shark who smells blood. He flies to the ball, intimidates, sets the tone. His dream is to make opponents remember his hits enough that they'll think twice about coming through the area again.

His leadership responsibility is enormous. He is the heart and soul of the defense. As the linebacker goes, so goes the rest of the team.

"I always knew I would play in this league. I had teams tell me I would have a hard time making it. They said I was a great player who had to get taller. I'd ask, 'What are you going to do, put me on the rack? What you see is what you get.' And that fueled the whole thing right there."

BARRON WORTHAM

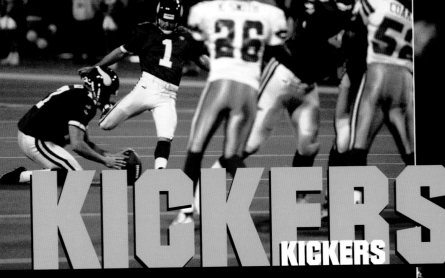

KICKERS

KICKERS

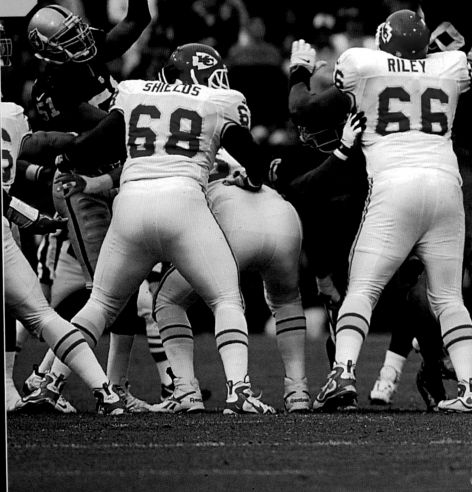

"People come up to me and say, 'Boy, with one second left in the game and in front of all those people, you have to go out there and kick that field goal. If you make it, the team wins. If you don't, the team loses. I could never do that!' And I say I could never do that without my faith. I realize that sometimes my job involves going out there with one second left and the game on the line."

GARY ANDERSON

Pressure. It defines a kicker.

His professional life hangs upon placing a 15-ounce, leather object packed with 13 pounds of air directly between two steel posts measuring only 18 1/2 feet wide. All with 70,000 rabid fans screaming at the top of their lungs. The kicker knows that every season, every game, each kick could be his last.

It's all about timing. Like the champion golfer, the kicker works hour after hour on his swing. Back swing, drive, follow through. Keep the head down. Again. Focus. Here, too, the "yips" can get to the best of them.

"It does lift the team when I'm kicking well and making the long ones. But if my self-worth was on the field, it would ride the ups and downs, and my value would depend on my field goals. That is a terrible way to live. I'm so glad that God never intended it to be that way."

JASON HANSON

QUARTER BACKS

"The best part of playing quarterback is the feeling after a big win. There's nothing like it. So much time and effort goes into each week. When you go into the locker room after a win and look at everybody who's involved in that success, and to be able to share it with them, that's the ultimate."

RICH GANNON

"The biggest thing I've learned is that the Lord has a plan for me. We don't always know what that plan is going to be or how we're going to get to where He wants us to be, but I've learned a lot along the way. I've learned about perseverance. I've learned a lot about being humble and being able to enjoy everything you get. I wouldn't change anything from the way it turned out. I've grown. I've become a better player and a better person through the experiences I've had. To be starting in the Super Bowl and to have won the MVP is stuff that you only dream about. You can't ever really think it's going to happen in your first opportunity. This is as good a script as I could have ever written."

"I've always believed in myself. I've always believed that I had the talent to get to this level and to be successful. I was just waiting for the opportunity. I was waiting for that door to open, to get a chance to prove to everybody that I could do it."

KURT WARN

"I'm sure nobody really expected me to get to the point where I am today, and you can't blame them. I think they were saying, 'This guy's working at a supermarket. How's he ever going to play in the NFL?' It's a strange story. I mean, if I was looking at it from the outside, I probably would have thought the same thing."

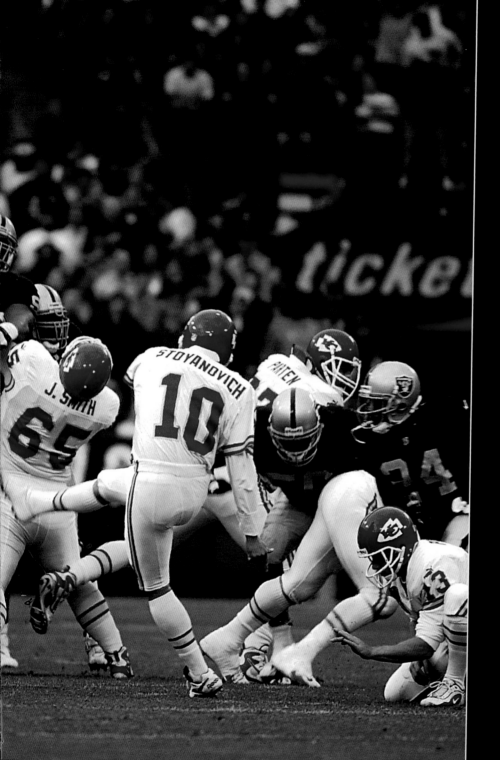

His craft is dependent on others. The snap from center
must be on target. The holder's placement must be at
the right angle with laces in front. All three men must
work to precision. If not, the onus is on the man with
the foot.

The kicker is a solitary figure. Aloof. He practices his
art alone, on the other end of the field from the rest of
the team. He longs simply to become one of the guys.
But when Sunday comes, he will again be found alone
on the sidelines, preparing for the inevitable. Best not
to get too close to men he might disappoint.

While for baseball hitters 30 percent is good, for
quarterbacks 60 percent is tops, and for basketball
shooters 45 percent is average, a kicker must be perfect
80 percent of the time or he'll be looking for a new job.
Yet eight out of ten merely earns him a pat on the head
from his mates—until he trots out there again, and his
future hangs in the balance once more.

DEFENSIVE BACKS

He is the last line of defense. At times, he is a player totally isolated.

John Donne said, "No man is an island." He obviously never met a defensive back. Corners and safeties are usually the loneliest men in the game, out by themselves.

Matched up against the fastest, quickest, niftiest men in the sport . . . in the world, it's one-on-one, head to head, you and I. Like two gunslingers at a standoff, they see who will be quickest on the draw.

Help is usually twenty yards away.

It's a matter of reading and reacting. Read the receiver's moves and the quarterback's eyes and react to the ball—all within a matter of tenths of seconds. A split second too late can be disastrous. The Chinese proverb says, "He who hesitates is lost." So it is for the defensive back—hesitation means your man is headed to the end zone.

"You don't play a sport to come in second place. God keeps putting me in the right place at the right time, and fortunately, I've been able to make my fair share of plays over the years. Being a child of God, you understand that you are a conqueror, you were placed here to do great things."

MERTON HANKS

JIM HARBAUGH

No one athlete in American sports so captures our attention as the quarterback. He is the cover boy, the product endorser, the single most adored and revered hero in the entire sports world.

The object of too much praise in victory, the subject of too much criticism in defeat, the quarterback is the most watched and analyzed figure in all of sports. He has the dream job.

"I've always believed the greatest form of leadership is through example. You don't talk it, you walk it. You live it."
BART STARR

"I would not trade one single situation I've been in so far in the NFL. And there's been some bad ones, some ugly ones, and I've made some huge mistakes. But God has orchestrated them perfectly and used every single one to mold me as a person. And through molding me as a person, He's going to mold me into a better football player, too."

TRENT DILFER

"He never promised me that they would never catch a ball on me. He never promised me that they wouldn't score a touchdown on me. Guys are going to catch balls on you. God has promised, 'I will be there.' And He said, 'Get back up. Line back up. Forget about the last play.' You have to look forward."

AENEAS WILLIAMS

"Whoever I line up on, I tell him it's not going to be an easy day. I'm letting him know right now, because they're only going be as good as I let them be. You win some and you lose some, but if you don't go into a game believing you're going to win, you already lost before you got out there on the football field."

RAY BUCHANAN

Like the lineman, the defensive back is recognized only when something goes wrong. Hold your man to no catches for forty straight plays and no one notices. If he gets by you on play number forty-one, you earn the nickname "toast," because you just got burned. But in his dreams, the defensive back never gets beaten. That only happens in nightmares.

Here the "game of inches" is most profound, often measured in fingertips. Interceptions and deflections can be crucial, but then again, so can pass interference.

For the defensive back, the island has become home. Challenge is his close friend. His response to both is what sets him apart from all other athletes on the field.

"I'm never satisfied with my performances because I know I can do better. I can help the team much more than I'm helping them. Not for self-gratification, but I can help the team."

"Money. Can it make you happy? No. Did Super Bowls make you happy? No. Do cars make you happy? No. Has jewelry made you happy? No. Have women made you happy? No. So what can give you the final peace that you've been missing, that you've been grasping for all your life? It's only the peace of God, and you know that that's free. It doesn't cost you anything."

DEION SAN

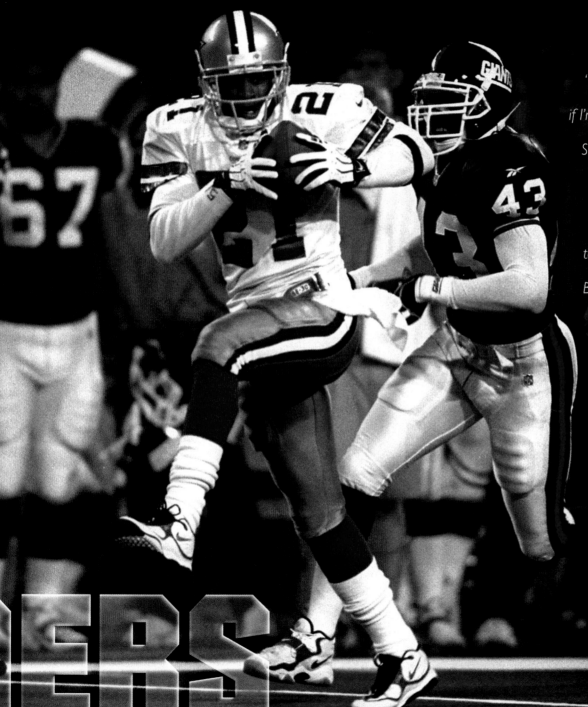

"I've always been the type of person who, if I'm going to do something, I do it 100 percent. Some people think Deion's going to be soft now that he's a Christian. He's not going to be prime time. Believe me, I'm going to be prime time when I step on that field. But I'm not going to do the evil things that I was doing when I step off that field."

"You make so many decisions as a football coach. We try very hard to make sure we get the right kind of character people. I think intelligence and character are two things in players that give you a better chance to have people who are going to be leaders and not followers."

DAN REEVES

COACHES

COACHES

Coaches are the game's brain trust. Their lives are spent shaping strategies and molding men.

Everything begins and ends with the coach. The commander in chief on football's battlefield, his men listen to him, carry out his orders, and rise to the level of his expectations. He is a master motivator, who inspires his players to individual achievement and, more importantly, corporate greatness.

"Winning and losing is obviously very important. That's what we get judged on. That's why we get paid. But you realize it's not the most important thing. We want to win games, but if that's all we do is win games, then I don't think we've done enough. We need to win in a first-class way. We need to win in the way that honors God, and do other things off the field as well as winning."

TONY DUNGY

"The chemistry that's involved in a team is really the bottom line. It takes special guys. It takes special team discipline."

CHAN GAILEY

Coaches who have become legends have had some things in common:

• They cared for their players and put the players first, never intentionally sacrificing the well-being of an individual for personal glory.

• They developed character in their players and staffs—not just within football, but also beyond the game.

• They were never jealous of nor overly awed by their star players; they knew how to handle a situation when a player received more credit than they.

• They were teachers as well as strategists and innovators of new schemes and plays.

• They were good human beings—humble in victory, gracious in defeat, kind to all.

• They were intent to never stop growing on a personal level.

"It has to be very clear to the team who the coach is. I believe in that. Yet at the same time, the football players get it done. It's their team. The players should receive all the credit."

MIKE HOLMGREN

"It's a people business. You don't win in football with Xs and Os and equipment. You win with people. When you get 50 or 60 people together in any endeavor, you're going to have problems, and you're going to have great success and thrills. It's one of the hardest things in the world, yet the only thing worthwhile in life, really, is people."

JOE GIBBS

Many coaches would make great military leaders. They are constantly discovering how to outthink their opponents, not waste manpower, keep casualties to a minimum, and teach courage as the one weapon in attack or defense that can't be destroyed. Many would be top CEOs. Ultimately, they realize success is not based on formulas and strategies, but on people.

Coaches are the final authority for their men. For many players they are father figures who are sought out for advice on life decisions, often late at night.

Their impact in an individual life goes beyond the playing field or locker room. What they instill in the players who call them "Coach"—through word and example—will be imbedded for a lifetime.

"We're in a very emotional, stressful, and, at times, volatile business. To be able to rely on someone else when things get tough is very important, because you really can't do it yourself. A lot of things are out of your control. A lot of things, maybe sometime later on you'll realize why they happened. So, just to keep your life in perspective is very important. That's what my Christianity does for me."

MIKE HOLMGREN

"To be a successful coach in the NFL you have to be able to respond to trials. You have to be able to respond to adversity. There's not a lot of positives in losing, but as long as you are learning from it, as long as you don't make the same mistakes twice and you're growing as you go."

TONY DUNGY

GAME PLAN

It is one of those phrases that has passed from sports into the mainstream of society. Game Plan. Have an ideal of where you are going and how you intend to get there. Evaluate the opposition. Study the problems. Prepare for the unexpected. Everything is possible, if only you have a game plan.

No coach would lead his men onto the field without a game plan. Each week, every step, every drill, every film session, every aspect of practice is all geared around the game plan.

The game plan is the sole focus of a team's preparation and execution. Know the game plan. Eat, drink, and sleep the game plan all week. On Sunday, execute the game plan, and success and victory will be yours. Stray from the game plan, and you are headed for failure.

"If my whole foundation is football, when the bad times come (and they do), where are you going to be?"

DANNY WUERFFEL

There's so much in this world that you can't control. We do things the hard way, try to do it ourselves. I'm constantly reminded that Kevin Carter can do nothing without Jesus Christ."

KEVIN CARTER

"I think life is making decisions and choices. Tough times are a part of life. And yet, by being a Christian and belonging to God, the promise is that in the end everything is going to work out the best for us. What a great promise that is! No matter what happens in my life, God is bigger than all that, and in the end it's all going to work out great for me."

JOE GIBBS

"People ask me, 'How can you not let the pressure get to you? How can you remain calm and not worry about what people are thinking?' It's Jesus Christ who lives in me that gives me peace. No matter what happens on the football field, even if I throw three interceptions and we lose, God will still be there for me, and He's got a plan."

DANNY KANELL

"It's like Romans 8:28 says: 'All things work together for good for those who love God and are called according to his purpose.' There have been a lot of things that at the time made no sense to me, but looking back now and seeing the total picture, it's amazing and awesome what God had in store."

BRUCE MATTHEWS

Life is much like a football game. Each day, each stage in our lives is like a play, a series of downs. Each season of life like a quarter.

A successful drive down the football field is made up of many plays strung together—some successful, some not so successful, but all combined to achieve a touchdown. There are sacks and yards lost along the way, perhaps an injury or two, but adversity doesn't stop the team on a scoring drive. They are focused on the goal line ahead.

Enough successful drives means, in the end, the scoreboard will read in your favor.

So it is with life. Adversity hits, we get sacked, execute poorly, or even fumble. Yet to win, we must press on. We need to see the ultimate goal and set our sights accordingly.

All football players have faith in the game plan. They know even if they are behind at halftime, if they don't panic but stick to the game plan, they can win the game.

"Knowing that God has a plan—that we are not here by accident, we are not mistakes—really drives me and enables me to go through the good times and the bad times. Because I know that overall God's plan is greater than anything I could plan out for myself."

JOHN MICHELS

"God didn't put me on the earth just to run up and down the football field."
DEION SANDERS

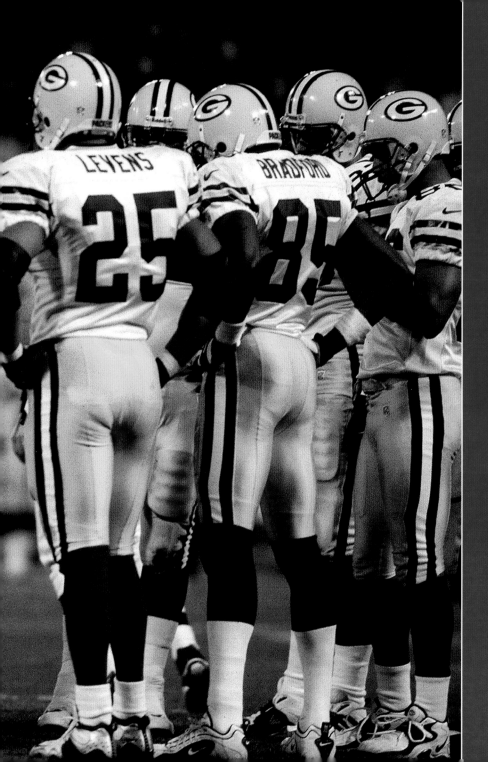

In life, many people find themselves at halftime with the scoreboard not looking so good. The players in this book know, however, that there is a "Coach," and He does have a winning "game plan." Getting on the same page of that game plan with "the Coach" will result in victory for all in life's biggest game.

For two quarters, three quarters, even at the two-minute warning, you might be behind. But the game plan is built for success at the end. It's never too late for that plan to work. A turnover, and momentum changes. A first down, a big catch, a great block, a missed tackle, a long gain, and suddenly you're in position to score.

In the heart of a champion, this is what playing the game is all about—seeing the scoreboard at the end of the game, with the score in your favor.

It's all according to the game plan. That's how "the Coach" drew it up.

"The key verses in my life are from Proverbs 3:5-6: 'Trust in the Lord with all your heart and lean not unto your own understanding, but in all your ways acknowledge Him and He will direct your path.' It gets real complicated here sometimes. I take a great deal of comfort in knowing that God is in charge of where we're going."
MIKE HOLMGREN

POST GAME

"A lot of guys talk the talk, but it's about walking the walk. My favorite verse is Philippians 4:13: 'I can do all things through Christ who strengthens me.' Life is about challenges. There's always going to be tough times. He's the Guy you have to talk to during those tough times. He'll give you the strength."

PEYTON MANNING

"What defines the heart of a champion is the desire to give your all and have no regrets about what you left behind. The Bible doesn't say run the race so that you achieve the crown. It says run the race in such a manner that you would achieve the crown."

JOHN MICHELS

"It's priceless. It's better than any touchdown, any long run, any game-winning catch. It makes all that worthwhile."

CRIS CARTER

"God is bigger than a football game, and He wants to touch people's lives. That's what my goal is, and this gives me a platform."

KURT WARNER

"When you think about Jesus' life on earth and what He did for us, it's the most beautiful thing that ever happened. And there are no strings attached."

MIKE HOLMGREN

"Success is knowing God. Success is having a relationship with Jesus Christ. The world defines success as money, popularity, and all that. In football, success is being the best at your position, having a bunch of endorsements, having a big contract. That isn't true success. Success is having a relationship with Jesus Christ, and personally that's where I find my success. That's where I find meaning in life. It's the contentment that comes from knowing that no matter what your circumstances are, you have meaning and fulfillment."

MARK BRUNELL

"I'm a firm believer that a lot of people think they're searching for happiness, but what they're really searching for is joy, and there's a difference. Happiness is based on your circumstances. I can tell you I'm not happy when my back hurts. I'm not happy that I've got 90 degrees range of motion in my knee. But I have a wife and three children who love me. I know Jesus loves me, and I know when I leave this planet I'm going to heaven. So, I have joy in my heart about that."

MARK SCHLERETH

"This is a short life—70 to 80 years at best. To know that we will spend eternity in heaven with God because we put our faith in Christ is the main promise in the Bible. What more comforting thing can there be than to know your eternal destiny."

KYLE BRADY

TOM LANDRY

"A lot of times through those years when I was on the sidelines and we had difficulties and problems, I felt God's presence with me. That made all the difference in the world, especially in how I reacted and how I handled people."

Tom Landry knew the final score.

When the legendary coach of "America's Team" died on February 12, 2000, he left a legacy that will be difficult to match. "America's Coach" knew the purpose for his 75 years was more than winning football games. Win he did, totaling 270 wins—third most in NFL history—over his 29 seasons, with a record 20 consecutive winning seasons. He led his Dallas Cowboys teams to five conference championships, 13 division titles, and 18 playoff births. His teams won two Super Bowls.

He was an innovator, responsible for developing the 4-3 defense, the "flex" defense, the multiple offense, shifts and motion, and restoring the spread or "shotgun" formation. His innovative mind, steely game face, meticulous preparation, and plaid fedora were all hallmarks of the man who walked the sidelines. But more than that, Tom Landry was devoted to developing people as winners beyond the game of football. All who knew him said he was a living example of the character of God. He touched hearts and changed lives

Those close to Coach Landry say he told them he was "ready" in the end. Ready for what would come next. Over a lifetime filled with success and innovation, Tom Landry knew he had finished the game. He sat under life's true "Coach," learned His strategies, studied His "game plan," and implemented what he had learned.

"The thing I discovered was that to have a right relationship with Jesus Christ is the most important thing. Your priorities must change. It's not enough just to go to church and sit in the pew. Your priorities have to change. And mine changed. God became first in my life, and my family became much more important to me. And, of course, football became third."

"When I got into coaching, he was the guy I looked up to … someone to pattern my career after. He was, first of all, a great person, and I think the Lord let him leave a great stamp on a lot of people. He was a rare guy."

"Coach Landry wasn't one to preach to you every day. He led his life. He walked the walk. He also had the vision of knowing that football wasn't the ultimate success, and that's the reason he became a Christian. The things that he talked about and showed in his life have helped me become a better person. Hopefully, I can have the influence on half as many people as Coach Landry influenced in his life."
DAN REEVES

"How could such a man grow to be so loved and respected by so many? Tom Landry's faith and deeds went hand in hand. That's why he was so beloved. He lived his faith every day in so many ways."
ROGER STAUBACH

"He was like my second father. He imparted principles and integrity and character in us that we probably lost when we went to college. When I went to that first meeting and he told me about his priorities—God, family, and football— I thought he was kidding."
BOB LILLY

"He made you want to follow him by example. I didn't understand what he was talking about back then. But while he was teaching us Xs and Os, he was teaching us about

"The real testament about Tom is that he'll teach us more now that he's gone than when he was here. We were learning from him and we didn't even know it

Honor Books
Department E
P.O. Box 55388
Tulsa, Oklahoma 74155

or by e-mail at: info@honorbooks.com

inspire a dream • inspire a dream • inspire a dream • inspire
dream • inspire a dream • inspire a dream • inspire a dream
nspire a dream • inspire a dream • inspire a dream • inspire
ream • inspire a dream • inspire a dream • inspire a dream
inspire a dream • inspire a dream • inspire
dream • inspire a dream • inspire a dream • inspire
nspire a dream • inspire a dream • inspire a dream • inspire
ream • inspire a dream • inspire a dream • inspire a dream
inspire a dream • inspire a dream • inspire